Learn the ABCs
Tt
Warren Rylands and Eric Doty
LIGHTBOX
openlightbox.com

LIGHTBOX

Go to
www.openlightbox.com
and enter this book's
unique code.

ACCESS CODE

LBXN2753

Lightbox is an all-inclusive digital solution for the teaching and learning of curriculum topics in an original, groundbreaking way. Lightbox is based on National Curriculum Standards.

OPTIMIZED FOR

- ✓ TABLETS
- ✓ WHITEBOARDS
- ✓ COMPUTERS
- ✓ AND MUCH MORE!

STANDARD FEATURES OF LIGHTBOX

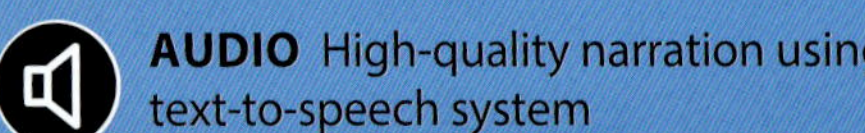
AUDIO High-quality narration using text-to-speech system

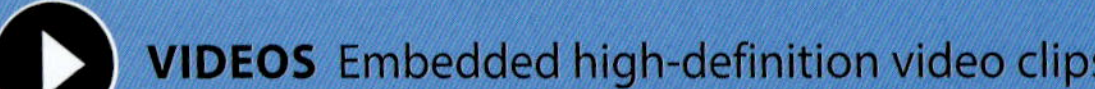
VIDEOS Embedded high-definition video clips

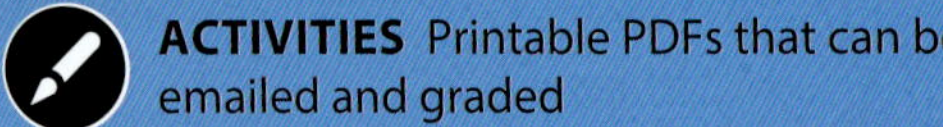
ACTIVITIES Printable PDFs that can be emailed and graded

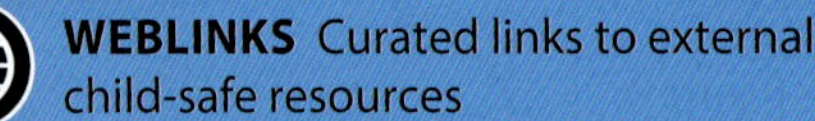
WEBLINKS Curated links to external, child-safe resources

SLIDESHOWS Pictorial overviews of key concepts

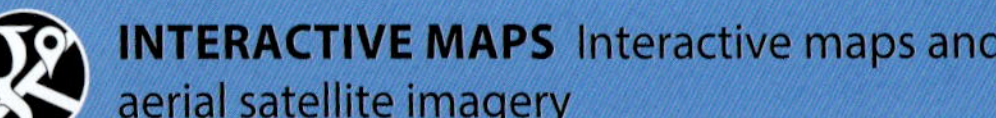
INTERACTIVE MAPS Interactive maps and aerial satellite imagery

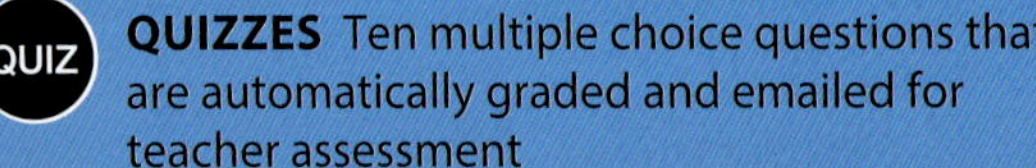
QUIZZES Ten multiple choice questions that are automatically graded and emailed for teacher assessment

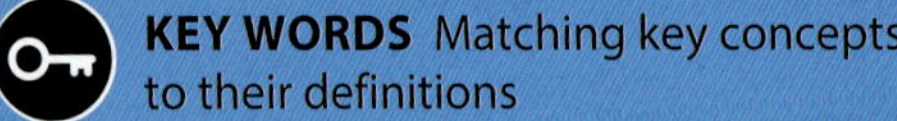
KEY WORDS Matching key concepts to their definitions

VIDEOS

WEBLINKS

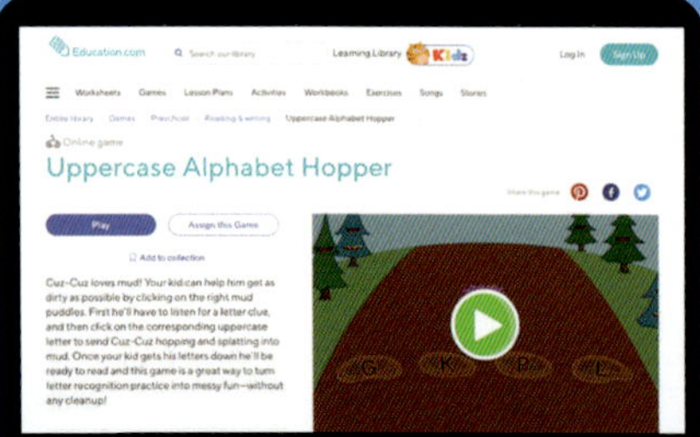

SLIDESHOWS

QUIZZES

Tt

CONTENTS

Let's discover the letter

Learn the ABCs

Tt

CONTENTS

Let's discover the letter

This is an uppercase T

This is how
you write it

This is a lowercase t

This is how
you write it

The letter t can start many words.

tiger

6023
turkey
tractor
tree

The letter t
can be inside
a word.
water
eating

enter

toothpaste

birthday

The letter t can be at the end of a word.

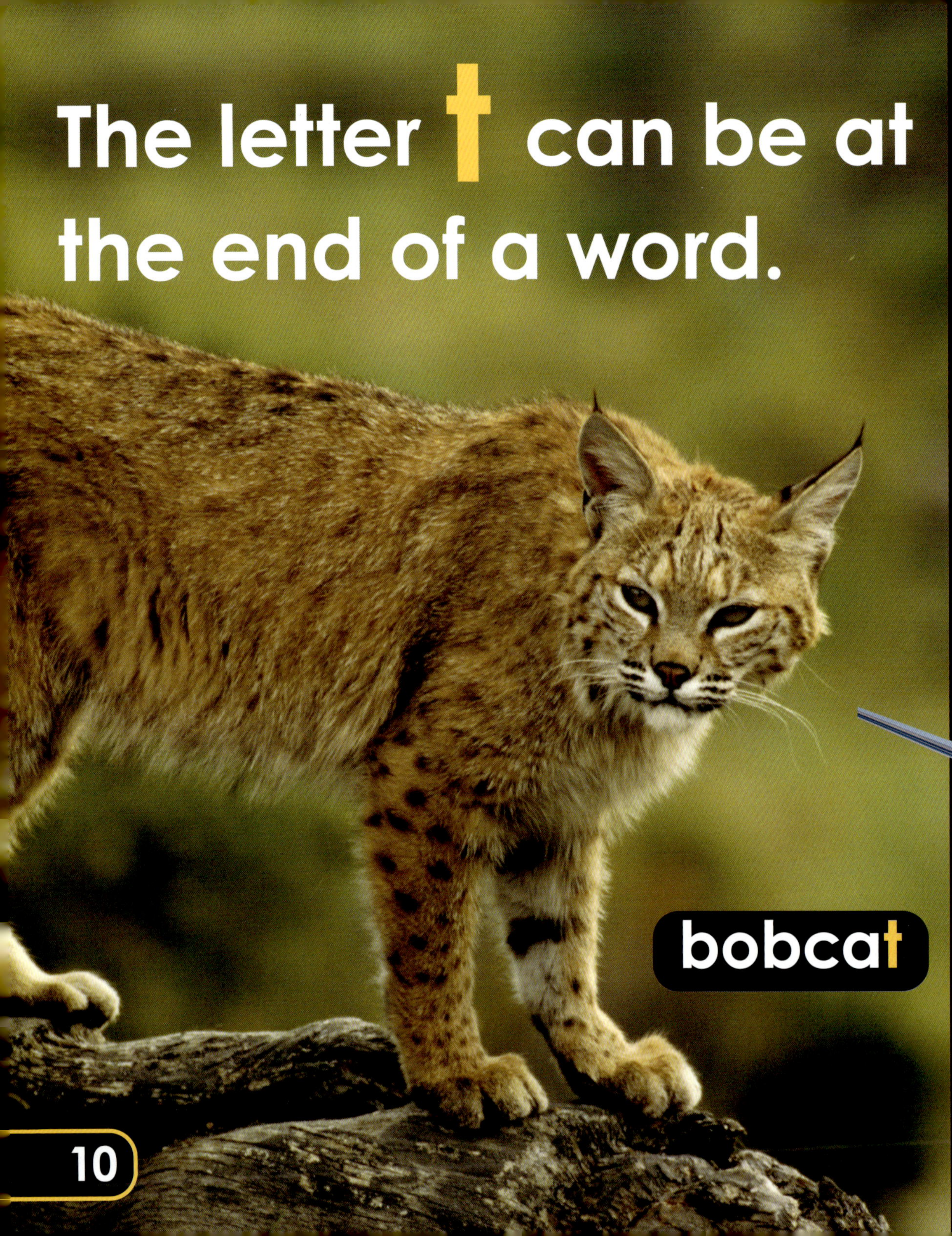

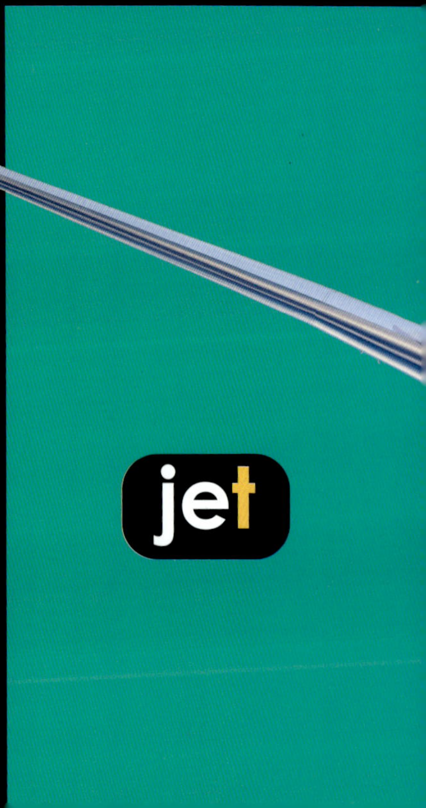

bobcat

jet

vet
ant

Many names start with an uppercase T.

Tammy sings a song.

Teresa does yoga.

Timothy saves money.

Terry can skateboard.

Thomas is tall.

The letter t makes different sounds.

tire

thumb

The letter t makes a t sound in the word **tire**.

The letter t helps to make the th sound in the word **thumb**.

The letter t makes a t sound in most words.

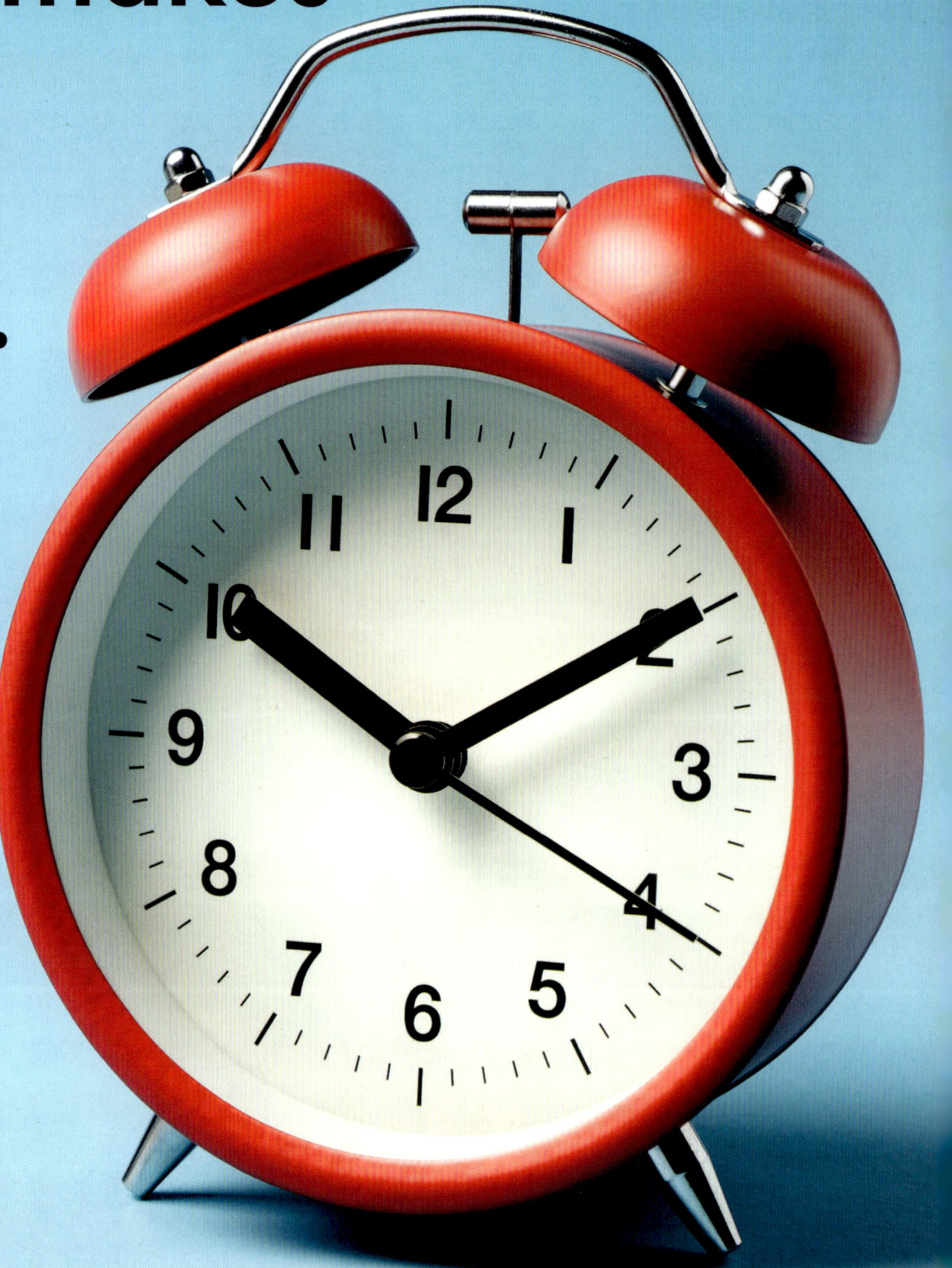

time

to
not
try
about

In other words, the letter t helps to make the th sound.

the
think
bath
mother

Having Fun with T

Terry often thinks about eating birthday cake. Birthday cake is Terry's favorite treat.

On Tuesday, Terry took the train to Tammy's town.

Tuesday afternoon is cake time in Tammy's town.

Tammy told Terry to bring three bobcats. The bobcats needed a bath!

Bobcats cannot eat with dirty feet!

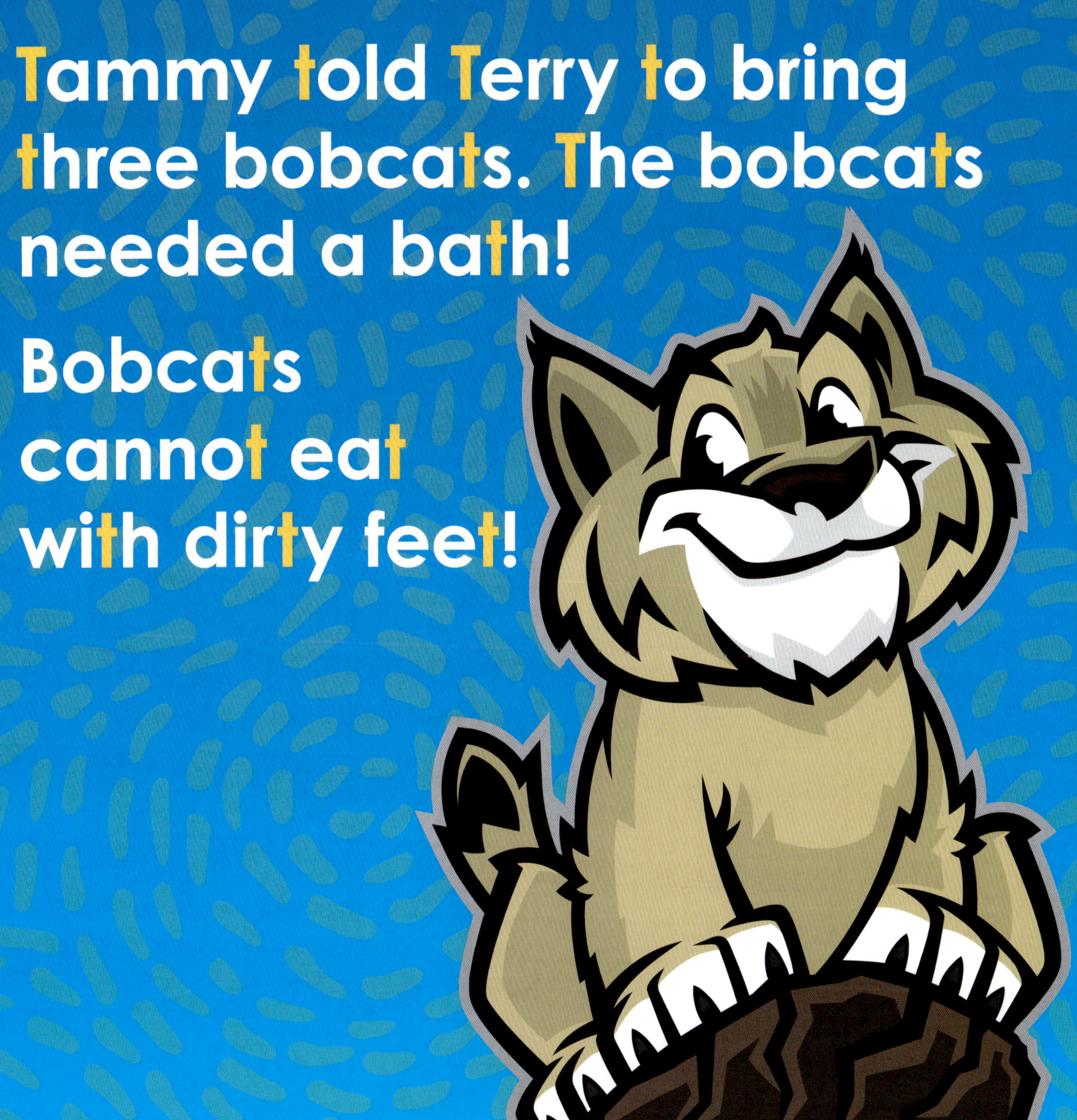

The alphabet has 26 letters.

T is the twentieth letter in the alphabet.

Aa Bb Cc Dd

Ee Ff Gg Hh Ii Jj

Kk Ll Mm Nn Oo

Pp Qq Rr Ss **Tt** Uu

Vv Ww Xx Yy Zz

KEY WORDS

Research has shown that as much as 65 percent of all written material published in English is made up of 300 words. These 300 words cannot be taught using pictures or learned by sounding them out. They must be recognized by sight. This book contains 46 common sight words to help young readers improve their reading fluency and comprehension. This book also teaches young readers several important content words, such as proper nouns. These words are paired with pictures to aid in learning and improve understanding.

Page	Sight Words First Appearance
4	let, letter, the
5	a, an, how, is, it, this, write, you
6	can, many, start, words
7	tree
8	be, water
10	at, end, of
12	names, song, with
13	does
14	different, makes, sounds
15	helps, in, to
16	most, time
17	about, not, try
18	other
19	mother, think
20	often, on, took
21	eat, feet, three
22	has

Page	Content Words First Appearance
4	Tt
6	tiger, train
7	tractor, turkey
9	birthday, toothpaste
10	bobcat, jet, pet
11	ant, vet
12	Tammy
13	money, Teresa, Terry, Thomas, Timothy, yoga
14	thumb, tire
18	feather
19	bath
20	afternoon, cake, fun, treat, town, Tuesday
22	alphabet

Published by Smartbook Media Inc.
276 5th Avenue, Suite 704 #917
New York, NY 10001
Website: www.openlightbox.com

Library of Congress Cataloging-in-Publication Data

Names: Rylands, Warren, author. | Doty, Eric, author.
Title: Tt / Warren Rylands and Eric Doty.
Description: New York, NY : Smartbook Media Inc., [2022] | Series: Learn the ABCs | Audience: Grades K-1.
Identifiers: LCCN 2020054166 (print) | LCCN 2020054167 (ebook) | ISBN 9781510557925 (library binding) | ISBN 9781510557949 (ebook other)
Subjects: LCSH: T (The letter)--Juvenile literature. | English language--Consonants--Juvenile literature. | English language--Alphabet--Juvenile literature.
Classification: LCC PE1165 .R9542 2022 (print) | LCC PE1165 (ebook) | DDC 421/.1--dc23
LC record available at https://lccn.loc.gov/2020054166
LC ebook record available at https://lccn.loc.gov/2020054167

Printed in Guangzhou, China
1 2 3 4 5 6 7 8 9 0 25 24 23 22 21

022021
110820

Art Director: Terry Paulhus **Project Coordinator:** Sara Cucini

The publisher acknowledges Getty Images as the primary image supplier for this title.